Big Cats Book of Amazing Pictures and Fun Facts About Big Cats

(Nature Books for Children Series)

By John Yost

ISBN 978-1495202506

Copyright © 2014

All rights reserved

Please respect my copyright of this book. You may use this book for your personal enjoyment. Just like a printed book, you may share it with family and friends. Please don't change or modify this book in any way though. Your personal license to enjoy this book doesn't extend to reselling or redistributing this book in whole or part for any other commercial purpose. In all other respects you are invited to enjoy and share this book with family, friends and other loved ones. Please spread the word and support the author by encouraging others to purchase and enjoy this book.

Table of Contents

Table of Contents 3

Introduction 5

Movement 8

Fur 10

Feeding 12

Senses 14

Roar...............................18

Bobcat 20

Cougar 24

Cheetah..........................29

Jaguar............................34

Leopard..........................38

Lion 43

Snow Leopard 48

Tiger 52

A Note From John 56

Introduction

Tigers usually hunt at night in the forests of Asia.

All big cats are mammals. A mammal is an animal that is warm-blooded, has a backbone and feeds its babies milk.

Big cats live on every continent except for Antarctica because it is too cold. They live in hot deserts, damp jungles, thick forests and some even live in snowy mountains.

Big cats are *nocturnal*. A nocturnal animal is more active at night than during the day.

Like housecats, big cats spend much of their day sleeping and lying around. At night they wake up to hunt or travel.

Baby cats are called *cubs* or *kittens*. Mother cats have their babies in homes called *dens* or other safe areas. Most cubs only stay with their mothers for about 2 years before going off on their own.

Movement

Cheetahs are the fastest animals in the world and can sprint up to 75 miles per hour!

Big cats are very athletic animals. They walk, run, climb and swim.

Some big cats, like cheetahs, run up to 75 miles per hour. They use their long tails for balance and to turn quickly.

They use their speed and agility to catch prey.

All big cats use their sharp claws and strong muscles when climbing trees and hunting other animals.

Unlike most housecats, most big cats like water. Some big cats that live in hot places cool off in rivers or ponds. Big cats also need to cross rivers. When traveling, they swim up to 18 miles in a day. That is over 240 laps in an Olympic pool!

Fur

This white tiger is one of most beautiful animals in the world.

Big cats have different colored fur that helps them stay hidden while they hunt. Many big cats have stripes and spots on their fur that makes them even harder to see.

Big cats that live in cold places have thicker fur to keep warm.

If you find a big cat where there it's cold and there's lots of snow, what color do you think its fur will be?

Feeding

This leopard caught a deer. Leopards drag their prey up a tree to eat so other predators don't steal their meal.

All big cats are *carnivores*. A carnivore is an animal that eats other animals.

Big cats sneak up on their prey then pounce on it or chase it down. They use their sharp teeth, claws and strength to attack.

After catching their prey, big cats move their food so other animals don't steal it. Cougars bury their food and leopards carry up a tree.

Big cats eat almost any animal that lives around them. They eat insects, snakes, fish, birds, monkeys, deer, zebra, sheep, buffalos and even crocodiles.

Most big cats are at the top of the food chain. This means other animals do not eat them.

Senses

Cats have excellent night vision. On the darkest night a leopard can see an ant crawl on the ground from 50 yards away!

Big cats have big eyes and see much better than people. They don't have to blink very much.

This helps when they are hunting because most prey animals are good at seeing movement.

Big cats see well in the dark. Their good night vision allows them to hunt at night.

Big cats have a third eyelid that closes from the side. If you have a pet cat, you might notice this eyelid when your cat first wakes up. It keeps the cat's eye moist without blinking.

All big cats hear very well. When they hear a sound, their ears move to hear the sound better. They know how far away an animal is just by hearing it.

Big cats have very sensitive noses. They smell about 14 times better than a human. They use their sense of smell to sniff out food or danger.

A cat can even smell with its mouth. It opens its mouth and raises its head to get a better whiff.

Every big cat has about 24 whiskers on its face. The whiskers are very sensitive and can feel nearby air currents. A cat doesn't have to see something to know it's there. The cat can tell if when it's next to something just from the change in airflow over its whiskers.

Roar

African lions are one of only four kinds of animals that can roar.

Only four kinds of big cats can roar: lions, leopards, tigers and jaguars. The funny thing is, big cats that can roar can't purr.

Big cats roar using special voice boxes in their necks.

People have voice boxes too but ours are not as powerful. Lions can roar as loud as 25 lawn mowers!

They roar to scare away other cats that are not friends. Lions make another kind of roar to tell other lions that are friends.

Bobcat

This bobcat moves silently through the snow in search of rabbits and rodents.

Most bobcats live in the United States, but there are some in Canada too.

They are called "bobcats" because of their short (bobbed) tails. Bobcats are also called "wildcats".

Bobcats spend their time in forests, swamps, deserts and sometimes even areas with houses!

Bobcats are grey, tan and brown. They have black spots and stripes. Their ears have black tufts of hair on top of them.

Bobcats are actually fairly small. They are only about 2 times the size of a housecat. In fact, bobcats aren't really big cats, but they are cool so I wanted to include them here for you.

Bobcats are nocturnal. If you see them during the day, it's probably because they need to find extra food for their babies.

Bobcats hunt by stalking their prey and then pouncing or ambushing it. They eat mostly rabbits and hares.

Bobcats are loners and live on their own instead of with other bobcats. They only get together to breed.

Bobcats hunt many animals. They catch and eat insects, squirrels, rodents, foxes, fish and mice. They will also eat bigger animals like sheep and deer if they find one that is already dead.

Cougar

This cougar rests peacefully during the day, waiting for night when it will travel and hunt.

Cougars live in the Americas: Canada, the United States and throughout South America. They are found in 11 different states in the United States.

The cougar is also called a "mountain lion" or a "puma."

Cougars are found in deserts, swamps forests and mountains.

Cougars are the fourth largest kind of cat. Male cougars weigh up to 220 pounds.

Cougars are born with spots and blue eyes. As they get older, their blue eyes turn yellow and their spots fade away.

Cougars can't roar but they make other noises. They hiss, growl and purr.

Did you know the cougar is not a lion even though it is called a "mountain lion"? It is actually more like a housecat than an African Lion.

Cougars are very athletic. They can jump from the ground straight up into a tree 18 feet high. They can also fall up to 65 feet without hurting themselves!

This lion leaps in the air as it attacks a rabbit in the snow.

Cougars are usually tan, brown, or red. Their fur is often thick to protect them from cold weather.

Cougars are also known for their loud screams. Although some people think that cougars scream when they attack another animal, their screams are actually used to attract mates.

Cougars are excellent at stalking their prey. They sneak up on sheep, deer, elk, moose and then pounce on them without a chase.

Cougars are near the top of the food chain, but there are some animals that eat cougars! Jaguars, black bears and grizzly bears all kill and eat cougars.

Cheetah

Cheetahs are the only big cat that can turn in mid-air while sprinting.

The cheetahs are the fastest land animals in the world. They can run up to 75 miles per hour!

Cheetahs live in Asia and Africa. They like deserts, savannas and prairies where there is thick brush.

Cheetahs are tan with black spots. The color of their fur helps them blend in with their surroundings when they hunt.

Cheetahs also have long, black stripes near their eyes called "tear lines." The tear lines keep the sun out of their eyes the same way football players use black strips under their eyes. Cheetahs can see prey from 5 miles away!

Cheetahs are very slim. They have long legs that help them run fast.

Cheetahs can travel 26 feet in a single stride. That's all the way across a street in one giant step!

Cheetahs can't roar. They purr and make sounds that might remind you of birds chirping.

These cheetahs drink at a waterhole in Africa. Even though it's hot where they live, they only have to drink every 3 or 4 days.

Cheetahs are the only big cats that don't have *retractable claws*. Retractable claws are claws that can be pulled inside the paw so they don't stick out all the time.

The cheetah's paws help it run fast. The claws give the cheetah a solid grip just like the spikes on a sprinter's track shoes.

After a cheetah captures its prey, it has to rest for hour to catch its breath before it eats.

Cheetahs eat different kinds of deer like springbok, gazelles and impalas. They also hunt wildebeests, zebras and rabbits. Unlike most big cats, cheetahs hunt more during the day than at night.

Jaguar

This female jaguar has to protect her cubs from other animals and won't even let their father near them.

The jaguar is the third biggest cat behind the tiger and African lion. Jaguars live in North America, Central America and South America.

They spend most of their time in rainforests, but they are also found in open areas.

A jaguar's fur ranges in color from light tan to jet black. They have black spots on their fur, but of course you can't see black spots on a black jaguar!

Jaguars have the shortest tails of any other big cat.

Jaguars are good hunters. They eat deer, mice, monkeys, turtles, cattle and even anacondas.

Jaguars live 12 to 15 years in the wild.

Even though it's only half the size of a lion, the jaguar's bite is twice as strong as a lion's! They can bite right through bones.

Jaguar cubs are born blind. They mature quickly and only stay with their mothers for about 2 years before going off on their own.

Leopard

This leopard wakes up in the evening to get ready to hunt during the night.

There are 12 different kinds of leopards. Leopards are found in African and Asia. They are more spread out in the world than any other big cat.

Leopards are the smallest of the big cats, but male leopards still weigh up to 200 pounds.

A leopard's fur can be light yellow, dark yellow, tan, orange, or black. They always have black spots. Just like black jaguars, sometimes you can barely see the spots.

Pound for pound leopards are the strongest of all the big cats. They often drag their kills into trees.

Leopards are the best climbers of all the big cats. They spend a lot of their time high in trees.

Leopards even hunt from trees and bring their food up with them. Sometimes they leave their food in trees so lions and hyenas don't steal their kill.

Usually leopards hunt from trees, but this leopard uses the grass to blend in as it sneaks up on its prey.

Leopards can go a whole month without drinking water. They get water from the animals they eat.

Leopards eat deer, warthogs, fish, monkeys, reptiles and even beetles. Leopards surprise their prey from high up in a tree or by hiding in a bush.

Leopards aren't very social. They spend their time alone instead of with other leopards.

Lion

This lioness and her cubs wait for the dominant male to finish eating before they have their lunch.

Lions are found mostly in Africa but some live in Asia. They are the second largest cat in the world. Some male lions weigh up to 550 pounds!

Even though they aren't the largest, lions are the tallest of the big cats.

There are only about 15,000 lions alive today. There used to be many more lions, but people have killed them. It's illegal to kill wild lions now, so hopefully the population will grow.

Male lions have a lot of fur around their faces called *manes*. Their manes make them look scary so other lions won't want to fight them.

Most lions have tan fur but a few have a white coat. Male

lions have tufts of fur at the end of their tails that are used to attract mates.

Lions are the only kind of cat that lives in a group. A group of lions is called a "*pride*".

A pride is like a family. There are usually about 30 lions in a pride. If hunting is good in an area, there can be 50 lions in one group!

Even though lions are considered the "The King of the Jungle", they spend most of their time in the open plains. These plains are called *savannas*.

A female lion is called a "lioness". The lioness hunts for her pride. Lionesses are smaller than male lions and do not have manes.

Even though this male lion and cub share in the meal, neither of them hunts. The lionesses do all the hunting for the pride.

While lionesses hunt, male lions guard the pride's territory and watch over cubs. If an intruder comes, the male will scare it away or fight it.

Lions hunt zebras, deer, wild pigs, impalas, gazelles, hippos and even elephants. They like to hunt at night.

Lions spend up to 20 hours a day resting. That is 90% of their entire lives!

An adult lion's roar is so loud that it can be heard up to 5 miles away. It is no surprise that their roar is the loudest of the big cats.

Snow Leopard

Snow leopards are one of the few cats that eat grasses and twigs in addition to other animals.

The snow leopards live in the icy cold mountains of China and Central Asia. They live where it's so cold that our blood would freeze in minutes. Less than 100 people have ever seen a snow leopard in the wild.

The snow leopard is the smallest of the big cats. They usually weigh less than 120 pounds but they look bigger because of their fur.

Snow leopards are different from other big cats because they live in the bitter cold and snow. They have large paws that are like snowshoes so they can walk on top of the snow without sinking in.

Snow leopards have huge, furry feet so they can walk on top of the snow instead of sinking into it.

Their fur is longer and thicker than any other big cat's. Their long fur helps keep them warm. A snow leopard's fur can be white, grey, tan or yellow with black spots.

Snow leopards also have the longest tail of any big cat. Their tails are almost as long as they are! Their long tails are full of fat. If a snow leopard doesn't catch any food for a long time, it uses the fat in its tail to stay alive.

Snow leopards can kill animals four times as big as they are. That would be like a grown person catching a bull with their bare hands. Snow leopards eat sheep, goats, marmots, rabbits and pikas.

Tiger

When it's really hungry, a Siberian tiger can eat 60 pounds of meat in one meal.

The tiger is the largest cat in the world. They are native to

Russia and Asia. In the wild they spend their time in grasslands and forests. But because people have hunted them so much, there are more tigers in captivity than there are in the wild.

The biggest tiger is the Siberian tiger, males weigh up to 670 pounds! They can also be up to 11 feet long from their nose to the tip of their tail.

Tigers have the largest canine teeth of any carnivore that lives on land. Do you remember what a carnivore is? If you said a carnivore is an animal that eats meat, you're right!

Most tigers have fur that is orange with black stripes, but some tigers have white fur with black stripes.

Tigers are great swimmers and can swim up to 3 miles. On land they can run 40 miles per hour!

A tiger's stripes are like people's fingerprint. Every tiger has a different stripe pattern. If you shaved all the hair off a tiger, you would still see the stripes on their skin.

Tigers hunt alone. They are so big that they can take down large animals like camels, bears and buffaloes.

Tigers love water and they are great swimmers. They are skilled hunters in water where they feed on fish and even crocodiles!

A Note From John

Dear Reader,

Thank you very much for reading my book on big cats. I get great feedback from teachers, parents and children who have enjoyed this book. I hope you liked it too!

If you did, please leave a 5 Star review on Amazon. Your review really helps me out a lot and is the probably the most appreciated thing you can do for me! :) You can leave your review by going to your Amazon account and clicking on your *Big Cats* book.

Big Cats is the third book in a series of *Nature Books for Children* that I'm researching and writing. Every time I write a book, I'm fascinated by what I learn. For example I think it's cool that snow leopards have wide, furry feet that work like snowshoes. Feet like that would have been nice growing up in the Wisconsin snow! I also didn't know that not all big cats could roar, or that you could hear a lion roar from 5 miles away! I love learning this stuff!

It's my hope that I can pass some of my love and

enthusiasm for nature on to you and your children.

I also write in hopes that your family enjoys reading these books and talking about them together; giving you the opportunity to teach strong values to your children and grow closer as a family.

And of course, I truly hope you are inspired to appreciate this beautiful world we live in.

Again, if you and your children have enjoyed this book, I'd like to ask you to leave a great review on Amazon. Reviews help others discover the book and I love knowing that I've given something to you and your family.

Thank you so much!

John

P.S. Feel free to write me to chat, give me ideas for new books, or tell me how I can make them better for you and your family. You can email me at johnnie.yost@gmail.com

P.P.S. Please visit my author page below to see what new books you and your kids can enjoy together!

http://amazon.com/author/johnyost

Made in the USA
Middletown, DE
29 November 2016